GE✴GRAPHY NOW!

COASTLINES

AROUND THE WORLD

JEN GREEN

D1539960

PowerKiDS
press™

New York

Published in 2009 by The Rosen Publishing Group Inc.
29 East 21st Street, New York, NY 10010

First Edition

Editor: Jon Richards
Designer: Ben Ruocco
Consultant: John Williams

Library of Congress Cataloging-in-Publication Data

Green, Jen.
  Coastlines around the world / Jen Green. — 1st ed.
      p. cm. — (Geography now)
  Includes index.
  ISBN 978-1-4358-2871-1 (library binding)
  ISBN 978-1-4358-2957-2 (paperback)
  ISBN 978-1-4358-2963-3 (6-pack)
  1. Coasts—Juvenile literature. I. Title.
  GB453.G74 2009
  551.45'7—dc22

                                      2008025802

Manufactured in China

Picture acknowledgments:
(t-top, b-bottom, l-left, r-right, c-center)
Front cover istockphoto.com/Doug Schneider, 1 istockphoto.com, 4-5 Dreamstime.com/David Coleman, 4br
stockphoto.com, 5br istockphoto.com/Karen Locke, 6-7 Dreamstime.com/Stuart Elflett, 6b istockphoto.com/
Leslie Banks, 7br London Aerial Photo Library/CORBIS, 8-9 istockphoto.com/Benjamin Schepp, 8b
Dreamstime.com/David Hughes, 9br Dreamstime.com/Kenneth Mellott, 10-11 istockphoto.com, 10bl
Dreamstime.com/Darryl Sleath, 11br Dreamstime.com/Publicimage, 12-13 istockphoto.com/Jay Spooner,
12bl istockphoto.com/Laila Røberg, 13cr istockphoto.com/Erik de Graaf, 13br istockphoto.com/Lya Cattel,
14-15 Dreamstime.com/Christina Deridder, 14bl istockphoto.com/Jan Kranendonk, 15br istockphoto.com/
Doug Schneider, 16-17 Richard A. Cooke/CORBIS, 16bl Dreamstime.com/Xavier Marchant, 17br
istockphoto.com/Mark Moquin, 18-19 istockphoto.com/Todd Taulman, 19cr courtesy of NASA,
19br Daniel Aguilar/Reuters/ Corbis, 20-21 Dreamstime.com/Debra Law, 20bl istockphoto.com, 21br
courtesy of U.S. National Oceanic and Atmospheric Administration, 22-23 Matthew Polak/Corbis Sygma,
23tr Dae Sasitorn/www.lastrefuge.co.uk, 23br Digital Vision, 24-25 Dreamstime.com/Philip Smith, 24bl
istockphoto.com/Daniel Breckwoldt, 25br istockphoto.com/Marisa Allegra Williams, 26-27 courtesy of NASA,
26cr Rafiqur Rahman/Reuters/Corbis, 27cb Dreamstime.com/Anthony Hall, 27br istockphoto.com/Eric Isselée,
28-29 istockphoto.com, 28bl Dreamstime.com/Bernard Breton, 29br Dreamstime.com/Alexander Putyata

CONTENTS

What are coastlines?

The coast is the boundary where dry land meets the ocean. Coasts form very long, narrow strips snaking around the edges of the world's continents and islands. Nowhere more than a few hundred yards wide, coasts run for over 530,000 miles (850,000 km) worldwide.

Some stretches of coastline are wild and undeveloped. Others are home to major cities, such as Sydney, Australia (below).

VARIED LANDSCAPES

The scenery found on the world's coastlines is extremely varied. Steep cliffs, sandy coves, mangrove swamps, or marshy deltas may be found there. These landscapes are formed when crashing water breaks up solid rock. The shape of the coastline is affected by factors such as the strength of waves and currents, and the hardness of local rocks.

A snorkeler (right) enjoys the clear blue waters of a coastal resort. Tourism is an important industry in many coastal areas.

CHANGING HABITATS

Coasts generally have a mild climate, called a maritime climate. They offer habitats to wildlife such as birds, seals, and mollusks. Many humans choose to live by coasts because they are rich in resources, such as food and minerals. Over the centuries, many coastlines have been developed, and large ports have grown up. Human settlements have put natural habitats at risk, however.

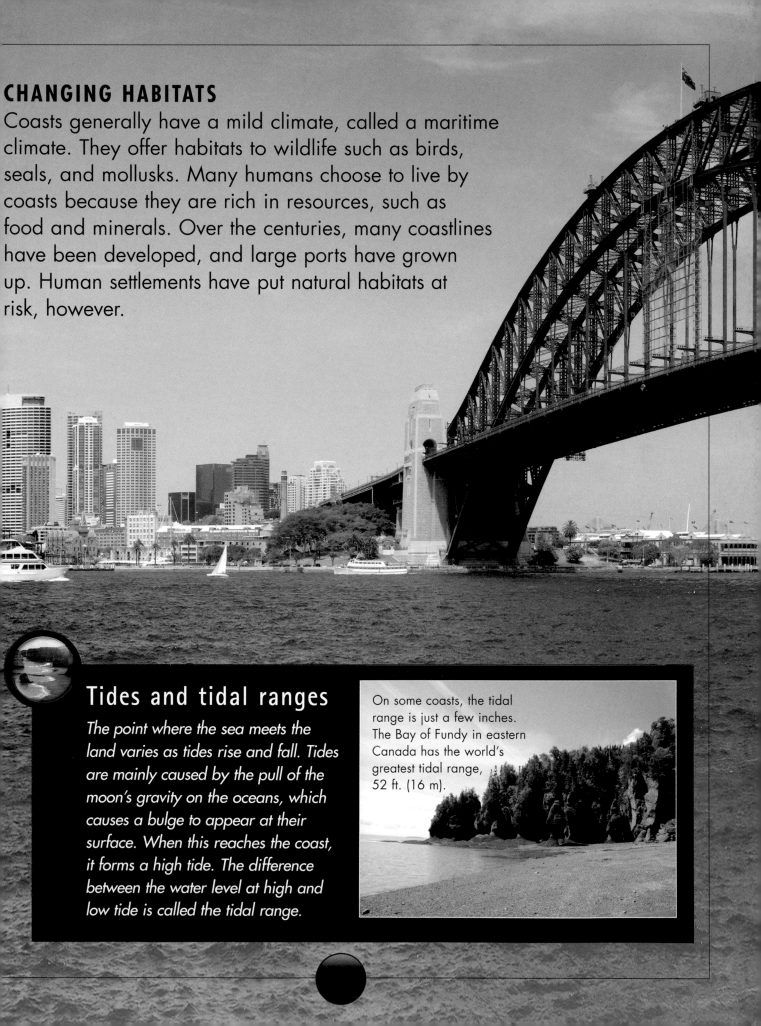

Tides and tidal ranges

The point where the sea meets the land varies as tides rise and fall. Tides are mainly caused by the pull of the moon's gravity on the oceans, which causes a bulge to appear at their surface. When this reaches the coast, it forms a high tide. The difference between the water level at high and low tide is called the tidal range.

On some coasts, the tidal range is just a few inches. The Bay of Fundy in eastern Canada has the world's greatest tidal range, 52 ft. (16 m).

Shaping coasts

The coastline changes constantly due to erosion and deposition. Erosion is the wearing away of the land by natural forces. Deposition occurs when the sea drops rocky debris onto the land.

EROSION

Waves cause erosion. As they crash on the shore, they force water and air into cracks in the rocks, slowly widening them. Waves also hurl sand and grit at the coast. These materials act like sandpaper, gouging away more rock.

Beaches form where rocky debris is deposited in sheltered spots, such as bays. The beach may be made of sand, rounded pebbles, or small stones called shingle.

DEPOSITION

While the sea erodes some stretches of coast, it builds new land in others. Coastal waters are full of rocky debris, either worn from seaside rocks or carried out to sea by rivers. Tides and currents carry the debris along the coast. It is dropped in areas of calm water, where it may form beaches, spits, or islands.

Headlands are formed when soft rock erodes, leaving harder rocks jutting out into the sea. When a narrow headland or rock arch collapses, it can leave a tall pillar, called a stack, in the sea (shown left).

Coastal retreat

Waves eat away at the base of cliffs to form a deep notch. Eventually, the rock on top collapses, and the coastline moves a little farther inland. This is called coastal retreat. In some places, the sea is eating into soft coastal rocks by a yard or more a year. Sometimes a whole section of cliff collapses at once.

Landslides usually happen during heavy rain or violent storms. This landslide occurred on the south coast of England in August 2000.

Changing sea levels

Sea levels are not only affected by daily tides. In the longer term, sea levels gradually rise and fall on coasts because of changes in climate. Over the last million years, scientists believe that sea levels have varied by up to 660 ft. (200 m), as long, cold periods called Ice Ages have come and gone.

Fjords, such as this one in New Zealand, are edged by high mountains, which plunge steeply to create deep water in the inlet below.

Rias, such as this one in southern Britain, are characterized by sheltered inlets, which were once the valleys formed by tributaries of a coastal river. These calm waters make good harbors for yachts.

ICE AND SEA LEVELS

During Ice Ages, sea levels are low. When the climate warms, the ice melts into the oceans, so sea levels rise. Since the last Ice Age ended around 15,000 years ago, sea levels have risen steadily. Features such as rias are evidence of flooding. Rias are estuaries that form when the sea floods a coastal valley.

DROWNED VALLEYS

The cycle of freeze and thaw can produce dramatic scenery on coasts. Fjords are steep-sided inlets with very deep water. They can be seen on the coasts of Norway, western Scotland, and New Zealand. Fjords began to form during Ice Ages, when coastal glaciers carved deep, U-shaped valleys. When the ice melted, the sea rose to flood valleys, creating fjords.

Rising waters

In the late 1900s, sea levels started to rise more rapidly. They rose by 2.25 in. (6 cm) in the last century, bringing increased risk of flooding to coasts worldwide. Scientists believe this is caused by rising temperatures, a problem known as global warming. Ice in the polar regions is melting, increasing the volume of ocean water.

This photo shows a glacier in Alaska breaking up, or calving. Large, floating pieces of ice, called icebergs, can choke polar waters and are a danger to ships.

Climate and wildlife

Conditions by the coast vary a great deal, but the sea's influence means that the climate is generally mild. The sea warms up more slowly than the land in the summer, and this keeps the coast cool. The sea also holds its heat for longer in the winter, keeping temperatures milder than those inland.

Wild cliffs are home to colonies of seabirds. They are good places to raise chicks, because they are beyond the reach of most

COASTAL HABITATS

Coasts provide many different habitats for wildlife, including cliffs, dunes, and salt marshes. On tropical coasts, lagoons, mangrove swamps, and coral reefs provide nurseries for fish and shellfish. Rocky coasts are home to limpets, crabs, and sea anemones. Worms, snails, and crabs live beneath the surface of mudflats and sandy beaches, providing food for gulls and wading birds.

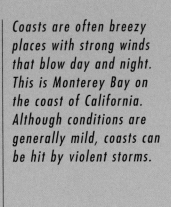

Coasts are often breezy places with strong winds that blow day and night. This is Monterey Bay on the coast of California. Although conditions are generally mild, coasts can be hit by violent storms.

HOT AND COLD CURRENTS

Coasts generally have high rainfall, because they lie in the path of moist ocean winds. Coastal climates are also influenced by warm or cool currents flowing offshore. For example, Britain is warmed by the balmy Gulf Stream current, which flows across the Atlantic Ocean from the Gulf of Mexico. In contrast, the coasts of Japan are cooled by a cold current flowing south from the Arctic.

Rockpool life

Rockpools on the shore are rich in wildlife, such as crabs, sea anemones, and small, slippery fish called gobies. Seaweed and algae provide food for plant-eaters such as winkles and limpets. Crabs, gulls, and starfish prey on the plant-eaters or scavenge dead creatures.

A rockpool teems with life, including seaweed, sea urchins, starfish, and sea anemones.

Using coasts

Coasts are rich in resources such as food and energy. The sea provides a means of transportation, and good farmland may be found near the water's edge. It is not surprising that over 20 percent of the world's population lives in coastal regions. In some places, the proportion is even higher—a third of people in Britain live near the coast.

Oil platforms can be seen in coastal waters in many parts of the world. Oil extracted from the seabed is either loaded onto tankers or pumped ashore.

FOOD, TRANSPORTATION, AND INDUSTRY

Coasts were first settled by humans in prehistoric times. People fished in the sea, and mild coastal climates provided good conditions for growing crops. Fishing villages grew into busy ports, and some became centers of industry, with factories processing materials brought by boat.

MINING AND TOURISM

From the mid-1900s, coastal waters became an important source of energy. Oil rigs were built to mine oil and natural gas from the seabed, and the energy of the wind and tides was harnessed. The same period saw the rise of tourism.

Tourism is now big business on many coasts. High-rise hotels line beaches, such as this resort in the Caribbean.

Port of Rotterdam

Some major ports have grown up not at the coast, but a short distance inland, on river estuaries. The Dutch port of Rotterdam lies about 19 miles (30 km) from the sea. Rotterdam grew quickly after the construction of a canal in the 1870s, which allowed seagoing ships to dock there.

Rotterdam handled more than 400 million tons of cargo in 2007, making it the world's third-busiest port.

Threatened coasts

Many of the world's coastlines are now well developed, with fishing ports, docks, and industrial areas, or resorts with hotels, shops, and marinas. Fishing, industry, and tourism can harm fragile coastal habitats, however. Conservationists work hard to protect the scenery and wildlife of coasts.

Litter is a problem on many beaches, even ones that are a long way from any port or city. Glass and plastic drift in with tides and currents, and pile up on the beach.

These fishing boats have anchored at Newfoundland. The cod fishing industry in Newfoundland had to shut down in the 1990s, because cod had become very scarce.

THREATS TO WILDLIFE

Fishing has been an important coastal industry for centuries. By the late 1900s, however, modern technology such as sonar had made fishing fleets so efficient that catches became unsustainable. Fish stocks plummeted, since too few fish were left to breed. Governments have now set strict limits on the numbers of fish that can be caught, to allow fish stocks to recover.

POLLUTION

Pollution is a problem along many coastlines. Coastal waters are polluted by waste dumped at sea, and also by chemicals from farms, factories, and settlements inland that are carried out to sea by rivers. Pollution can harm marine life. People can also be affected if they eat polluted seafood. Most coastal nations now follow strict international rules controlling the amount of waste that can be dumped at sea.

Preventing erosion

In some places, the coast itself is threatened, as the sea eats into the land. Concrete sea walls, high banks called dikes, and boulders heaped along the shore can absorb the energy of the waves and so protect the coast. Other stretches are left wild, for waves and currents to take their course.

The sea is wearing away the coast at Martha's Vineyard, off the Massachusetts coast, by 5.6 ft. (1.7 m) each year, one of the highest rates of coastal erosion in the world.

Rugged coastline

Hawaii

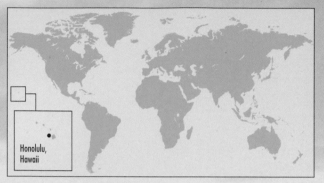

Honolulu,
Hawaii

STATISTICS

- Location: Central Pacific
- Coastal features: Include high cliffs, beaches of volcanic sand
- Climate: Tropical/oceanic
- Population: 1,211,500 (Hawaiian chain)
- Main industries: Tourism, farming
- Environmental issues: Introduction of nonnative species threatens local wildlife

The coastal landscapes of the islands of Hawaii in the Pacific Ocean are varied and often dramatic, ranging from towering cliffs to idyllic beaches. These landscapes were formed mainly by uplift—when the land is forced upward by powerful forces inside the Earth—and erosion.

SHEER CLIFFS

Sea cliffs form where high ground meets the ocean. The cliffs on the Hawaiian island of Molokai are the world's highest, rearing 3,315 ft. (1,010 m) above the waves. The islands of Hawaii were created by volcanic activity. Like most remote islands far out in the ocean, they are really the tips of massive, cone-shaped volcanoes rising from the ocean bed.

Whale-watching is a fairly new tourist activity. On Hawaii, small craft carry tourists out into coastal waters to view humpback whales.

SETTLEMENT AND INDUSTRIES

Hawaii's first inhabitants were the Polynesians, who reached the islands by canoe over 1,000 years ago. They settled on the coasts and lived by fishing, farming, and rearing livestock. Hawaii's main industry is now tourism. Since the 1960s, cheap air travel has allowed vacationers from around the world to visit these remote islands.

The cliffs of Molokai rise steeply from the ocean. Here, moist ocean winds create lush vegetation. The Hawaiian chain consists of eight large islands and over 100 smaller ones, spread out over 1,500 miles (2,400 km) of the Pacific Ocean.

Sand and surf

Many tourists come to Hawaii to laze on beautiful beaches of volcanic sand. The pounding waves have smashed volcanic rocks such as basalt into a fine powder. Hawaii is also renowned for its surfing. On the island of Maui, surfers ride waves up to 60 ft. (18 m) high—among the world's biggest.

Waves are formed by winds blowing across the sea surface. The shape of the seabed off the coast of Maui causes waves to rear up and spill over into high, curling crests.

Beach resort

Cancún

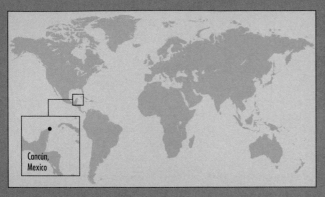

Cancún,
Mexico

- Location: Gulf of Mexico
- Coastal features: Sand spit backed by lagoon
- Climate: Tropical/maritime
- Population: 526,700 (2005)
- Main industry: Tourism
- Environmental issues: Erosion, pollution, habitat loss

Sandy beaches are the type of coastline most popular with tourists. Cancún on Mexico's Yucatán Peninsula is one of the best-known tourist spots on the Gulf Coast—yet just 50 years ago, this lively resort was a wild, empty strip of shore.

Cancún grew rapidly, partly with the help of foreign investment. Hundreds of hotels now line the shore.

DEVELOPMENT OF CANCÚN

The resort of Cancún lies on a slender spit of white sand stretching out into a blue ocean. In the 1970s, developers realized this beautiful place would make a perfect resort. A string of hotels and swimming pools was built along the shore. Highways, bridges, and an airport were constructed to connect the site with the Mexican mainland and allow access from abroad.

ENVIRONMENTAL COSTS

Four million tourists visit Cancún each year. The growth of what is now a major town has harmed habitats such as lagoons, dunes, and nearby forests. Coastal species such as seabirds have lost breeding sites. Sewage and detergent from hotels pollute the water. Hotels also deplete the local water supplies.

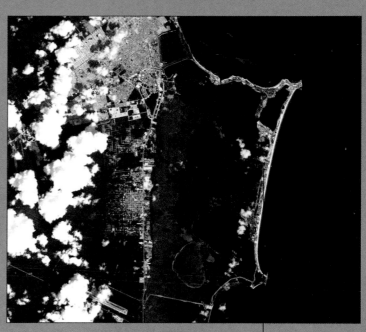

This satellite image shows the spit of Cancún sticking out from the Yucatán Peninsula. The spit is packed with hotels and backed by its lagoon.

Hurricane risk

Tropical resorts such as Cancún are at risk of hurricanes in the summer season. These giant spinning storms form out at sea in warm, sticky weather, and cause havoc when they hit the coast. In 2005, Hurricane Wilma struck Cancún with winds of over 150 mph (240 kph), causing over $4 billion in damage.

Damage from Hurricane Wilma. The hurricane swept away much of the beach, which had to be restored using sand dredged from 19 miles (30 km) offshore.

Coral reef coast

Great Barrier Reef

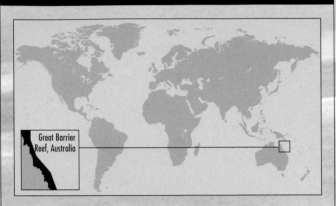

Great Barrier Reef, Australia

STATISTICS

- Location: Coral Sea, off northeastern Australia
- Coastal features: Barrier reef running parallel to coast
- Climate: Dry tropical
- Nearest coastal towns: Cairns, Townsville
- Main industry: Tourism
- Environmental issues: Warming sea temperatures

Coral reefs are very special coastlines. They form in clear, shallow waters off shores in the tropics. The Great Barrier Reef off northeastern Australia is the world's longest coral reef, stretching for over 1,250 miles (2,000 km). It is made up of more than 2,000 separate reefs.

REEF HABITATS

Several different types of coral reef are found worldwide. On some tropical coasts, they run along the edge of the shore, forming what are called fringing reefs. Barrier reefs form some distance out to sea and run parallel to the coast. The Great Barrier Reef is formed from over 350 different types of coral. It is home to 1,500 species of fish and thousands of species of mollusks, sponges, sea anemones, and shrimps.

Coral reefs are a very rich coastal habitat, home to more species of plants and animals than any other type of coast.

An aerial view of a small part of the Great Barrier Reef. This natural structure is so huge that it can be seen from space.

THREATS TO CORAL REEFS

Some of the world's coral reefs are under threat. Fishermen use dynamite to kill or stun schools of fish, and local people break off coral to sell as souvenirs. Sewage can pollute the clear waters that the coral need to survive. The Great Barrier Reef is protected from many of these dangers, because it is the world's largest marine park. However, it is still vulnerable to some hazards, such as coral-eating starfish and warming sea temperatures, which harm the coral.

Coral polyps

Coral reefs resemble rock, but are actually the chalky remains of billions of coral polyps. The polyps live on shallow coastal rocks in large colonies. They use minerals in the water to make chalky skeletons to protect their soft bodies. Over thousands of years, these skeletons build up to form the reef.

Coral polyps—relatives of sea anemones—open at night to capture scraps of food in their stinging tentacles. They withdraw inside their chalky shells by day.

Industry and pollution

Milford Haven

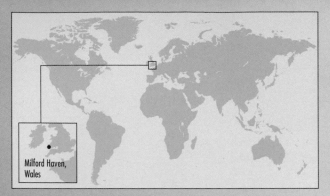

Milford Haven,
Wales

STATISTICS

- Location: *Pembrokeshire coast, south Wales*
- Coastal features: *Ria with deep-water harbor*
- Climate: *Temperate*
- Population: *14,000 (2005)*
- Main industries: *Oil refining, petroleum products*
- Environmental issues: *Pollution from industry*

The port of Milford Haven in south Wales is located on a ria, or drowned estuary. The deep, sheltered waters make a fine natural harbor. Once a fishing port, Milford Haven became a major center for oil refining in the 1960s. However, the oil industry brought environmental disaster in 1996.

A large oil slick spreads across the sea following the wreck of the Sea Empress in 1996. The clean-up operation cost a total of $120 million.

OIL SPILL

Even the biggest oil tankers are able to dock at Milford Haven, thanks to the inlet's deep waters. In 1996, a tanker named the *Sea Empress* approached the port laden with crude oil. Powerful tidal currents pushed the ship onto a rocky reef in the center of the estuary. Some 72,000 tons of crude oil spilled into the sea in one of Europe's worst oil disasters.

An aerial view of the refineries at Milford Haven. The estuary forms a small pocket of industry on what is otherwise a mainly wild coast.

THE CLEANUP

The port of Milford Haven is surrounded by the wild, rocky coastline of the Pembrokeshire National Park. The oil polluted 60 miles (100 km) of coastline. A cleanup operation was launched immediately. Small boats dropped floating booms to contain the slick at sea, while clean-up work began on the beaches. In the end, waves and currents helped to break up and disperse the oil.

Rescuing oiled birds

Seabirds were the most obvious casualties of the oil spill. When a bird's feathers are clogged with oil, the bird loses its natural waterproof coating and may quickly die of cold. At an emergency center, volunteers cleaned the birds' plumage with soapy water. After several days of recovery, the birds were released.

A bird struggles ashore with its feathers covered in oil. An estimated 20,000 birds were killed by the *Sea Empress* oil spill, along with thousands of fish and mollusks.

Threatened by the sea

Venice

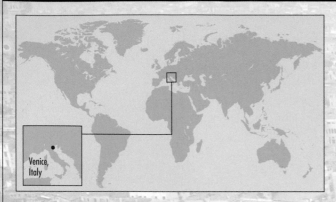

STATISTICS

- Location: Adriatic coast of Italy
- Coastal features: City founded on islands in a lagoon
- Climate: Temperate/Mediterranean
- Population: 270,250 (2004)
- Main industries: Tourism
- Environmental issues: Flooding, subsidence, pollution

The city of Venice lies just off Italy's northeast coast. The capital of a wealthy empire in medieval times, it is now a major center for tourism. However, Venice is under threat from the very force that once made it powerful—the sea.

A GLORIOUS PAST

Venice is built on over 100 small islands in a lagoon off the Italian coast. Established in the fourth century CE, the original foundations were wooden piles (stakes) driven into the swamp. In medieval times, the city grew rich through trade and became the capital of an empire that controlled the eastern Mediterranean. Wealthy merchants and bankers built beautiful churches and palaces.

A view of one of Venice's most famous churches, Santa Maria della Salute. The small craft on the canal are called gondolas.

SINKING CITY

Venice is unique. Instead of roads, the city is crisscrossed by canals that act as highways for gondolas and other boats. There are over 400 bridges. This beautiful city is sinking, however. It subsided (sank) by over 9 in. (23 cm) in the last century. Corrosive seawater is eating into the foundations of buildings, and alleys and squares are flooded during very high tides.

An aerial view of Venice's picturesque waterfront. Behind the tall belltower is St. Mark's Square, with St. Mark's Cathedral to the right.

Saving Venice

Several conservation schemes have been launched to save Venice and its art treasures. Now a multi-million-dollar engineering project is planned to protect the city. Inflatable barriers are set to be laid on the bed of the lagoon. Before very high tides, the barriers will be inflated to keep tidewater out of the city.

Tourists walk on wooden boards as a high tide floods St. Mark's Square. Planners hope the new sea defenses will be ready by 2011.

Earth's biggest delta

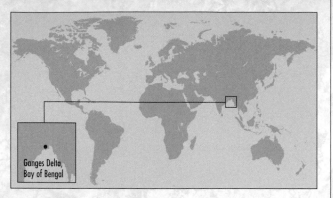

Ganges Delta

STATISTICS

- Location: Bay of Bengal, India/Bangladesh
- Coastal features: River delta with many channels/islands
- Climate: Tropical monsoon
- Population: Up to 140 million people
- Main industries: Farming, fishing
- Environmental issues: Flooding, overcrowding, pollution

Ganges Delta, Bay of Bengal

Deltas are flat, marshy areas at river mouths. They are made of silt, which is fine sediment dropped by the river as it reaches the ocean. The Ganges Delta is the world's largest delta, covering 28,970 sq miles (75,000 sq km). It measures 217 miles (350 km) wide where it meets the Bay of Bengal.

Floods contaminate river water, making drinking water scarce. Thousands in the Ganges Delta lined up for water during a flood in 2004 (right).

POPULATION AND WORK

One-third of the Ganges Delta lies in India. The rest is in the low-lying country of Bangladesh. Fertile silt and the tropical climate make the region ideal for farming. The main crops grown are rice, tea, and jute. Fishing is another major industry. About 140 million people inhabit the delta. With over 520 people per square mile in many areas, this is one of the most densely populated places on Earth.

This satellite image of the Ganges Delta shows the river splitting into many channels as it reaches the sea.

AT RISK FROM FLOODS

The whole of the Ganges Delta is at great risk from flooding. Summer rains often cause the River Ganges to burst its banks. The coastal zone is often hit by floods during cyclones (hurricanes). These giant storms suck up water and then sweep ashore. In 1970, Cyclone Bhola killed about a million people. The Ganges flooded in 1998, destroying 30 million homes.

Delta wildlife

The delta region includes the Sundarbans, the world's largest coastal mangrove forest. Mangrove trees are able to live in semisalty water. Fish called mudskippers skitter over the mud at low tide. Asian elephants, clouded leopards, crocodiles, crabs, and the rare Bengal tiger also inhabit the delta.

Delta wildlife includes the endangered Bengal tiger and the fiddler crab, which has one giant claw.

Ice-choked coast

Ross Ice Shelf

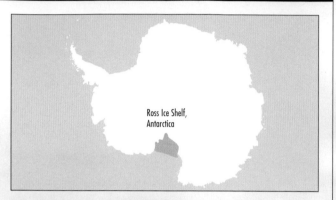

Ross Ice Shelf, Antarctica

STATISTICS

- Location: Antarctica
- Coastal features: Floating ice shelf fills a vast bay
- Climate: Polar/maritime
- Population: About 1,000 scientists in McMurdo Base
- Main industries: Scientific research, some offshore fishing
- Environmental issues: Melting coastal ice

Polar coasts look very different from other coastlines. Ice dominates the landscape. Glaciers flow down from high ground to the ocean, where they form huge floating ice shelves that stretch out to sea. The Ross Ice Shelf covers an area the size of Spain.

Emperor penguins breed in large colonies on Antarctic coasts. These hardy birds are well adapted to deal with the cold.

ANTARCTIC WILDLIFE

The Ross Ice Shelf is a vast triangle of ice covering 188,030 sq miles (487,000 sq km). Antarctica has the coldest, windiest climate on Earth, but the ocean makes the climate milder so coasts are warmer than places far inland. No animals can survive inland, but coasts teem with wildlife, including seals, penguins, and albatrosses. Shrimplike krill abound in the sea, providing food for fish, squid, and whales.

SETTLEMENTS AND WORK

People have never settled anywhere on Antarctica. In 1959, the Antarctic Treaty set the whole continent aside for conservation and scientific research. Scientists live on bases, of which the largest is McMurdo Base at the edge of the Ross Ice Shelf. About 1,000 scientists live here in the summer. Antarctica has rich mineral resources, but mining is not allowed and fishing in coastal waters is carefully controlled.

Ice cliffs rear 50–164 ft. (15–50 m) high at the seaward edge of the Ross Ice Shelf. However, 90 percent of the floating ice mass lies below the water.

Studying ice

Studies of Antarctic ice have revealed traces of pollution from distant regions. There are no farms or factories on Antarctica, yet pollutants have been found in the ice. Global warming is starting to melt ice at the coasts. In 2003, a section of ice the size of Belgium broke off and floated away.

These scientists are studying ice in an iceberg. Samples from deep below the surface of the ice cap show what the climate was like long ago.

Glossary, Further Information, and Web Sites

BAY
A curving inlet on the coast.

COASTAL RETREAT
When the sea eats into coastal rocks, so that the shoreline moves gradually farther inland.

CORAL POLYP
An anemonelike creature with a chalky shell.

CORAL REEF
A large structure found in tropical seas that is made from the skeletons of dead coral polyps.

CURRENT
A regular flow of water in one direction.

CYCLONE
Another word for a hurricane.

DELTA
An area of flattish land at a river mouth, formed by mud or sand dropped by the river as it reaches the sea.

DEPOSITION
When rock is dropped by wind or water to form new land.

DIKE
A bank built to prevent flooding.

EROSION
The gradual wearing away of the Earth's surface by wind, water, or ice.

ESTUARY
The mouth or lower stretch of a river, regularly washed by salt-water tides.

FJORD
A steep-sided inlet formed when the sea floods a glacier-carved valley.

GLOBAL WARMING
A general rise in world temperatures, caused by a buildup in the atmosphere of gases that trap the Sun's heat, which is causing sea levels to rise.

ICE AGE
A long, cold period in the Earth's history, during which ice covered more of the land than it does today.

LAGOON
A coastal lake that is separated from the sea by rocks or a spit.

MARITIME CLIMATE
The regular pattern of coastal weather.

MONSOON
A wind that changes direction annually, bringing heavy rain in certain months.

RIA
A drowned estuary formed by a rise in sea level.

SEDIMENT
Loose particles of rocky material, such as sand or mud.

SILT
Fine rocky particles that have been ground down to form clay, sand, or mud.

SONAR
Device that uses sound waves to measure ocean depth or detect shoals of fish.

SPIT
A slender finger of land stretching out into the sea.

STACK
A pillar of rock standing out to sea.

TIDAL RANGE
The difference in sea level between high and low tide.

UNSUSTAINABLE
When so much of a renewable resource is used that the resource dwindles.

UPLIFT
When the land is raised up by the powerful forces that build mountains.

FURTHER READING

Geography Fact Files: Coastlines
by Michael Kerrigan
(Smart Apple Media, 2004)

Precious Earth: Saving Oceans and Wetlands
by Jen Green
(Chrysalis Education, 2004)

WEB SITES

Due to the changing nature of Internet links, PowerKids Press has developed an online list of Web sites related to the subject of this book. This site is updated regularly. Please use this link to access this list:
www.powerkidslinks.com/geon/coastli

Coastlines topic web

Use this topic web to discover themes and ideas in subjects that are related to coastlines.

GEOGRAPHY
- How coastal landscapes are formed.
- How the forces of erosion and deposition shape coasts.
- Different types of maritime (coastal) climate.

SCIENCE AND THE ENVIRONMENT
- Climate change and how sea levels are affected by it.
- Environmental problems such as pollution, litter, and overfishing.
- Conservation work to tackle various environmental problems.
- The protection of coasts through the construction of sea defenses.

ART AND CULTURE
- Myths, legends, and stories about coastal peoples, including islanders, and the sea.
- Art, music, and culture of coastal cities, such as Venice, New York, Hong Kong, and Singapore.

COASTLINES

ENGLISH AND LITERACY
- Accounts of the lives of coastal inhabitants and people who work on coasts.
- Eyewitness accounts of disasters such as storms, hurricanes, and tsunamis (large waves).
- Debate the pros and cons of development on coasts— for example, building new resorts.

HISTORY AND ECONOMICS
- How people use coastal resources such as fishing, minerals, and energy.
- The development of ports and cities on coasts and estuaries.
- World shipping routes and the growth of trade.

Index